MYSTERIOUS PYRAMIDS

Giza: *Pyramids of Ancient Egypt*

Murray "Oak" Tapeta

A Crabtree Crown Book

Crabtree Publishing
crabtreebooks.com

Teaching Tips for Caregivers:

You can help your child learn by encouraging them to read widely, both as a leisure activity and as a way of satisfying their curiosity about the world. Reading helps build a strong foundation in language and literacy skills that will help your child succeed in school. This high-interest book will appeal to all readers in intermediate and middle school grades.

Use the following suggestions to help your child grow as a reader.

- Encourage them to read independently at home.
- Encourage them to practice reading aloud.
- Encourage activities that require reading.
- Establish a regular reading time.
- Have your child ask and answer questions about what they read.

Teaching Tips for Teachers:

Engage students throughout the reading process by asking questions like these.

Before Reading

- Ask, "What do you already know about this topic?"
- Ask, "What do you want to learn about this topic?"

During Reading

- Ask, "What is the author trying to teach you?"
- Ask, "How is this like something you have read or seen before?"
- Ask, "How do the text features (headings, index, etc.) help you understand the topic?"

After Reading

- Ask, "What interesting or fun fact did you learn about the pyramids of Giza?"
- Ask, "What questions do you still have about these ancient pyramids? How could you find the answers?"

TABLE OF CONTENTS

A PUZZLE FROM THE PAST

The world is full of mysterious places that hold the secrets of lost **civilizations**. Ancient ruins are like snapshots in time. They provide us with important clues about what life was like long, long ago.

Pyramids usually served as grand burial chambers for royalty or as temples for religious ceremonies or both. These structures exist in various forms around the world, built by civilizations that had little or no contact with one another.

The Pyramids of Giza were built from giant blocks of limestone. Originally covered in smooth white limestone and colorful granite, these outer casings have almost entirely disappeared. The stone casings were worn away by ***erosion****, cracked by earthquakes, and taken by builders over the centuries for new construction elsewhere.*

PYRAMID STYLES

The ancient Egyptians built pyramids in different styles throughout the ages as tombs for royalty and important people. The earliest pyramids were step pyramids, built with layers of terraces. Within 100 years, the Egyptians had engineered the true, smooth-sided style of pyramid. The three pyramids of Giza are true pyramids.

Built during the 26th and 25th centuries BCE, no one is exactly sure what methods were used to build them. Their massive stones were probably moved with sleds, rollers, levers, and ramps. A single block could weigh up to 15 tons (14 metric tons).

Tikal - Step pyramid

Giza - True pyramid

- 2600 BCE — Giza
- 2500 BCE
- 2100 BCE — Ziggurat of Ur
- 2000 BCE
- 900 BCE — Tikal
- 259 BCE — Qin Emperor

Teotihuacán - Talud-tablero pyramid

Ziggurat of Ur - Step pyramid

Borobudur - Step pyramid

Qin Emperor - Buried flat-topped, step pyramid

BUILT TO IMPRESS!

Why did so many different ancient cultures build similar towering shapes? Relying on the forces of nature, ancient builders learned that the taller you build, the bigger you had to make the base. This helped distribute the weight more toward the bottom so a very tall structure would not topple over.

210 BCE

100 CE

Teotihuacán

450 CE

778 CE

Borobudur

850 CE

900 CE

LIFE IN ANCIENT EGYPT

Five thousand years ago, the ancient culture of Egypt flourished on the banks of the Nile River. Most Egyptians were farmers. Over many centuries, powerful kings, called **pharaohs**, ruled the country. The throne was passed down from father to son. Ancient Egyptians worshiped many gods and believed in an afterlife. They believed the body and soul had to stay together after death to go on to the afterlife. Egyptians developed a way to preserve bodies called mummification. Pyramids were built as tombs for the **mummies** of pharaohs and important people. The Pyramids of Giza are the resting places of three pharaohs: Khufu, his son Khafre, and grandson Menkaure.

Although not a pyramid, one of the most famous discoveries in modern times was the burial tomb of King Tutankhamun in 1922 CE. It was remarkable because it had been undisturbed by grave robbers, and the young king's mummy was still inside. His tomb was filled with astounding treasures meant to support him in the afterlife. Carvings and colorful murals painted on the walls acted as a key that helped **archaeologists** unlock what life was like in ancient times.

*Today, thanks to **forensic** tools such as laser scanners and CT scans, scientists can now uncover the secrets of mummies without removing a single piece of cloth.*

TOO HUGE TO HIDE

While many monuments built by ancient civilizations were buried or hidden by forests over centuries, this is not true of the three Pyramids of Giza. With nothing but the sands of the Sahara Desert surrounding them, these gigantic monuments have been visible ever since they were built. Located on the Nile River, in Giza, Egypt, near the large city of Cairo, the impressive structures are unmistakable.

FIRST OF ITS KIND

The oldest known pyramid in the world was built in Egypt in the 27th century BCE. Located at Saqqara, the tomb is a step pyramid erected for Pharaoh Djoser. It probably started as a simple **mastaba** and was enlarged over the years. His tomb was empty of his mummy and any treasures that might have been buried with him.

The tombs of the three pharaohs were likely packed with precious offerings and items to be used in the afterlife. However, the tombs were empty when **excavated** in modern times. The burial chambers of Khufu and Khafre each contained a **sarcophagus**, but neither contained a mummy.

A mummy was found in Menkaure's tomb but modern carbon dating determined the body was significantly younger than the pharaoh. In 1838, Menkaure's beautifully carved sarcophagus, claimed by an **Egyptologist**, was lost in a shipwreck on its way to England.

THE GREAT PYRAMID

The oldest and largest pyramid in Giza is the pyramid built for Pharaoh Khufu. It is also known as the Great Pyramid. Each side of its square base is 756 feet (230 meters) long. With its original outer casing of smooth white limestone, it stood 481 feet (146 meters) tall. The entire pyramid is estimated to weigh nearly six million tons (5.4 metric tons). It was the most **colossal** structure built on Earth in its time. It is the oldest and only remaining structure of the Seven Wonders of the Ancient World.

Historians estimate that construction of the Great Pyramid lasted for 27 years. It involved tens of thousands of workers. It contains about 2.3 million limestone blocks. Each of the four sides of the Great Pyramid face one of the four points on a compass: north, south, east, and west. Unlike the highly decorated tomb of the much later king, Tutankhamun, the smooth granite walls inside the Great Pyramid are bare.

The pyramid builders were not slaves but laborers. Forensic analysis of the workers' skeletons buried near Giza show they were fed well and buried with respect. The bones showed signs of wear, breaks, and ***arthritis****, proving that building pyramids was hard work!*

The Great Pyramid was built to honor Pharaoh Khufu and serve as a tomb that reflected his royal status. Construction began around 2550 BCE, shortly after his reign began. Pharaohs typically began building their eventual resting places as soon as they ascended the throne to prepare in advance for the afterlife. Other than an ivory statue and a diary of commercial trade, no records survive that describe Khufu or his reign. Although Greek historians who lived 2000 years after Khufu described him as a **tyrant**, the pharaoh was remembered in Egypt as a wise ruler.

Pyramids are mostly solid stone inside with open spaces for burial chambers and passageways that lead to them. The Great Pyramid has two long, narrow passageways that lead to two rooms given the names the King's Chamber and the Queen's Chamber. The King's Chamber still contains Khufu's granite sarcophagus, but no mummy was ever found. A tunnel carved into the pyramid by grave robbers suggests that whatever was inside was taken long ago.

Pharaoh Khufu

Pharaoh Khufu's Granite Sarcophagus

The pyramid holds many mysteries, including secret chambers and locking systems using large stones to prevent grave robbers. Today, special robots help explore still-hidden areas to unlock more of the pyramid's secrets.

THE PYRAMID OF KHAFRE

The second-largest pyramid in Giza was built by Khufu's son, Khafre. Khafre inherited the throne after his father's rule. Construction of his pyramid began around 2520 BCE. It was originally 471 feet (143 meters) tall. It stands out from the others because part of its smooth limestone casing can still be seen on the outside at the top. Khafre's pyramid was built on higher ground than Khufu's, with steeper walls. This makes it look like it is larger than the Great Pyramid.

Next to the **causeway** that connects Khafre's valley temple and **mortuary** temple is the impressive Great Sphinx. Taller than a six-story building, it is one of the largest sculptures in the world and is carved mostly out of solid rock. By the 1800s, only its head was visible. The sand was cleared away to reveal the figure with the body of a lion and the head of a pharaoh. The face was likely carved to look like Khafre.

The Great Sphinx

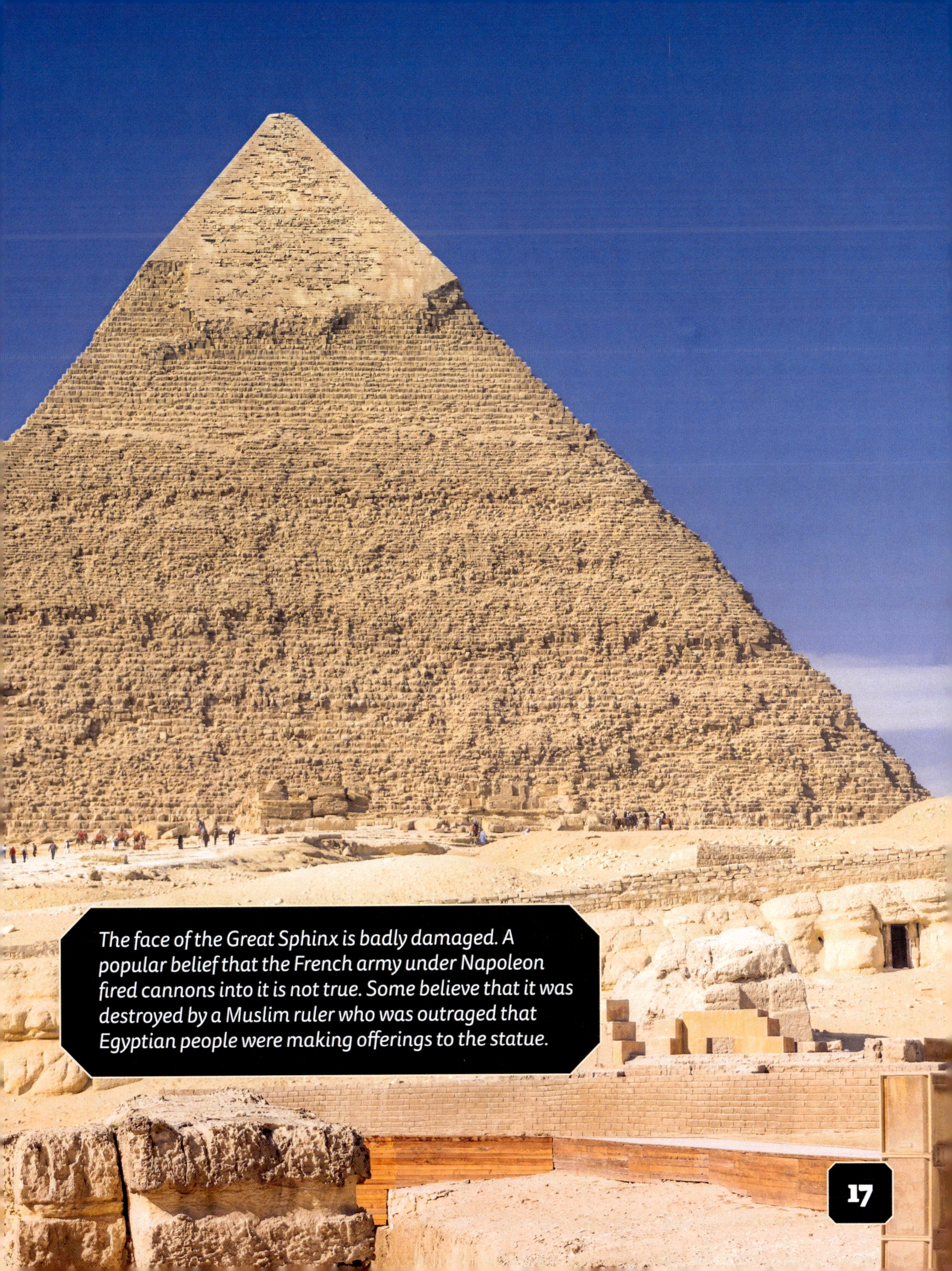

The face of the Great Sphinx is badly damaged. A popular belief that the French army under Napoleon fired cannons into it is not true. Some believe that it was destroyed by a Muslim ruler who was outraged that Egyptian people were making offerings to the statue.

THE PYRAMID OF MENKAURE

The third pyramid in Giza was built by Khafre's son Menkaure around 2490 BCE. At an original height of 218 feet (66 meters), it is much smaller than the other two. Unlike the other two pyramids, the walls of one of the chambers are lined with beautifully carved panels.

Although empty, insets in the walls suggest there may have been statues inside the pyramid. Statues of Menkaure were found in the mortuary and temple buildings attached to the pharaoh's pyramid. One statue found shows the pharaoh standing with his queen. Other statues show him with the goddess Hathor and a **personification** of the region of Thebes.

This statue shows Menkaure with the goddess Hathor on his right and a personification of Thebes on his left.

A large gash appears on the outside of Menkaure's pyramid from an attempt to destroy it by a sultan of Egypt in the late 12th century. A large crew worked for eight months, but they were no match for the solidly built structure.

TEMPLES

Each pyramid in Giza is linked to two temples. A mortuary temple near the base of the pyramid was a place for people to make offerings to the pharaoh in the afterlife. There were statues of the ruler, storerooms, and false doors to allow the deceased pharaoh to come and collect the offerings.

Each mortuary temple is connected by a long causeway, or road, to a valley temple closer to the Nile River. Some experts think these temples were built to allow pharaohs to visit the river in the afterlife.

Boats or models of boats have been found in pits near the mortuary temples in Giza. Some may have been used during the pharaohs' funerals. Others may have been provided for the pharaoh to use in the afterlife.

MORE TO SEE IN GIZA

There are other impressive structures at Giza. A number of tombs and mastabas stand near the pyramids. Queens were most likely buried here and not in the main pyramids. Here, the pharaoh's family members and important officials would be close by to counsel and serve the ruler in the afterlife.

Archaeologists also found the ruins of a small city. Pyramid building often took decades, so the houses might have belonged to the pyramid builders. Some of the buildings were bakeries.

STOLEN HISTORY

While there have been some attempts throughout the centuries to preserve ancient monuments in Egypt, treasure hunters, Egyptologists, and archaeologists began actively digging in Egypt in the 1800s. Over the last few centuries, explorers from other countries took Egyptian objects back to their own countries to be displayed in museums and personal collections.

The pyramids and temples in Giza likely contained countless rare and valuable **artifacts**. Most treasures were lost to grave robbers, probably in ancient times soon after the pyramids were sealed. Eventually, the ancient Egyptians began to hide the tombs of their pharaohs to prevent theft. It worked in the case of Tutankhamun. In 1922, thousands of years after his death, archaeologist Howard Carter discovered Tutankhamun's unmarked tomb mostly undisturbed. It still held its treasures inside—as well as the mummy of the pharaoh himself!

This bust of Queen Nefertiti is in a German museum.

Rosetta Stone

In 1983, the government of Egypt created the Egyptian Antiquities Law which declared all undiscovered artifacts belonged to Egypt. Any ancient **relic** found could not be owned in private collections or taken out of the country. The government is also pursuing the return of important artifacts held in the museums of different countries around the world. The most famous example is the Rosetta Stone, held in the British Museum for more than 200 years.

GUESTS OF GIZA

Tourists riding camels in Giza Plateau

Tourists from around the world flock to Giza to see the pyramids. Over 14 million people each year brave the desert heat to visit these amazing structures. Visitors can enter each pyramid and climb to the chambers. They can walk near the Great Sphinx as it stands guard while the desert sun rises and sets.

Archaeologists continue to carefully excavate the area. In 2023, they used scanning technology to discover a hidden chamber in Khufu's pyramid. That same year, several important tombs were unearthed on the site. Researchers continue to discover clues that help tell the story of three ancient pharaohs and their remarkable pyramids.

THE PYRAMIDS UNDER THREAT

Most images you see show the Pyramids of Giza surrounded by desert. But if you turned and looked in the other direction, you would see the city of Giza within walking distance of the Sphinx. Encroaching cities are one of the problems threatening this important heritage site. Increasing local populations and tourism lead to increased traffic, which means more air pollution impacting the stone of the pyramids. Heritage supporters have been fighting the building of a new highway too close to the pyramids and a possible multi-lane tunnel underneath the Giza Plateau.

In 1979, the Pyramids of Giza were added to the UNESCO World Heritage List. This organization works to protect unique historical and cultural sites considered important to the entire world. UNESCO has organized regular investigations of the pyramids to update their status and make recommendations on how to minimize threats and restore damage to the site.

Giza is a suburb of Egypt's capital city Cairo, whose **metropolitan** area is home to over 20 million people.

GLOSSARY

archaeologists (ahr-kee-AH-luh-juhsts) Scientists who study the distant past by digging up things that people made, used, and left behind

arthritis (ar-THRIGH-tuhss) Diseases that cause inflammation, pain, and swelling in the joints

artifacts (AHR-tuh-fakts) Objects made and used by humans in the past, including tools and weapons

causeway (KAWZ-way) A raised walkway used to cross wet ground

civilizations (siv-uh-li-ZAY-shuhnz) Groups of people with their own language and way of life

colossal (kuh-LAH-suhl) Extremely large

Egyptologist (ee-jip-TOL-uh-jist) A person who studies ancient Egypt's history, language, and culture

erosion (ih-ROH-zhuhn) The wearing away of soil or rock by natural forces, such as water, wind, or ice

excavate (EK-skuh-vayt) To dig up or uncover

forensic (fuh-REN-sik) Relating to scientific tests or methods used when investigating crime

mastaba (muh-STAH-buh) An early style of tomb used by the ancient Egyptians that is rectangular and has sloped sides and a flat roof

metropolitan (met-ruh-POL-uh-tuhn) Relating to a large city and its surrounding areas

mortuary (MOR-choo-air-ee) Relating to burial or tombs for the dead

mummies (MUHM-eez) Dead bodies that have been preserved with special chemicals and wrapped in cloth, especially by ancient Egyptians

personification (per-son-i-fi-ca-tion) The representation of an abstract quality, concept, or thing in human form

pharaoh (FAIR-oh) A king of ancient Egypt who was considered to be a god

relic (REL-ik) An object from an earlier time kept due to significance, respect, or historical interest

sarcophagus (sahr-KAH-fuh-guhs) A stone coffin

tyrant (TIE-runt) A powerful, cruel, and unfair ruler

INDEX

AFTER READING QUESTIONS

1. The youngest pyramid in Giza is _____.
   a. The Pyramid of Menkaure
   b. The Pyramid of Khafre
   c. The Pyramid of Khufu
2. The largest pyramid in Giza is ______.
   a. The Pyramid of Menkaure
   b. The Pyramid of Khafre
   c. The Pyramid of Khufu
3. The only pyramid in Giza that still has its original smooth casing is ______.
   a. The Pyramid of Menkaure
   b. The Pyramid of Khafre
   c. The Pyramid of Khufu
4. Grave robbers did not disturb the tomb of ____.
   a. Menkaure
   b. Khufu
   c. Tutankhamun
5. The face of the Great Sphinx probably looked like ______.
   a. Pharaoh Khufu
   b. Pharaoh Khafre
   c. Pharaoh Menkaure

Answers: 1. a, 2. c, 3. b, 4. c, 5. b

ABOUT THE AUTHOR

Murray "Oak" Tapeta was born in a toilet-less cabin in Montana. Growing up in the great outdoors, he learned to love trees. He got the nickname "Oak" after climbing to the top of an oak tree when he was only three years old. Oak loves to read and write. He has written a number of books about fascinating, terrible, and gruesome events from the distant past. He prefers spending time in the wilderness with his dog, Birchy.

Author: Murray "Oak" Tapeta

Editor: Kathy Middleton

Proofreader: Crystal Sikkens

Design: Samara Parent and Kathy Walsh

Production coordinator: Candice Campbell

IMAGE CREDITS

Shutterstock: ©Mohammed_Al_Ali, p 7 (second from top); ©CK-TravelPhotos: p 18 (bottom), p 21 (top); ©onapalmtree: p 20-21; ©Priscila. Perazzolo: p 24 (bottom); ©NorthSky Films: p 24-25

Wikimedia Commons: ©EditorfromMars: p 8-9; ©Olaf Tausch: p 14 (bottom)

All other images from Shutterstock

Crabtree Publishing

crabtreebooks.com **800-387-7650**

In Canada: We acknowledge the financial support of the Government of Canada through the Canada Book Fund for our publishing activities.

Hardcover 978-1-0398-7281-3
Paperback 978-1-0398-7339-1
Ebook (pdf) 978-1-0398-7394-0
Epub 978-1-0398-7443-5

Published in Canada
Crabtree Publishing
616 Welland Avenue
St. Catharines, Ontario
L2M 5V6

Published in the United States
Crabtree Publishing
347 Fifth Avenue
Suite 1402-145
New York, New York, 10016

Library and Archives Canada Cataloguing in Publication
Available at Library and Archives Canada

Library of Congress Cataloging-in-Publication Data
Available at the Library of Congress

Printed in the U.S.A./CP052026